Resilient Life

Resilient Life

Your Journey From Bitter Reality

to Hopeful Living

Bruce McIntyre

Printed in the United States of America

ISBN 978-0-615-19420-2

Published by Rabbit Ranch Press
A Division of Creative Life Studios, LLC
Oklahoma City, Okla.

Cover design by Tim Watson
www.visualinventor.com

Subject Headings: SPIRITUAL
MOTIVATIONAL
SELF-HELP

For more information about Resilient Life products and resources:
www.MyResilientLife.com

Dedication

This journey book is dedicated to my wife, Kathy. She is simply the best person I have ever known. Together, we continue to discover, learn, and embrace the resilient life. This book exists because of her.

Contents

Acknowledgements

I like to think of myself as a rather independent soul. In many respects, I am. I tend to help others much more than accepting help *from* others.

One cold morning in Columbia, Mo., in 2006, I walked through our neighborhood praying for God's guidance. The answer came quickly and stopped me abruptly on the sidewalk. *I needed help.* That was the truth.

With a sick wife and two pre-school children, I simply could not do it on my own. We were all suffering from my need to be independent.

Since that day, I have sought and graciously received much help from others. Joe and Belinda Kemp, my in-laws, invited us to live with them for a season of support. That season lasted longer than I had ever anticipated, and I can truly say that I have the best in-laws in the world. Roy and Dorothy McIntyre, my parents, helped us tremendously and especially in the early stages of our life crash with encouragement, concern, and practical help. Words fall far short in my attempts to describe my gratefulness for such good parents.

Jason Jones, Lance Robertson, Randy and Renee Grau, Jena Barocio, and Rev. Chip Hunter all provided crucial guidance and helpful critique as my Research and Development Team. Wyatt Fenno and David Loftis also graciously listened to my ideas and offered helpful feedback.

Jason McWilliams at Impressions Printing was extremely patient with me in helping create a good finished product. Tim Watson, owner of Visual Inventor, captured the idea of resilience in graphic form. My best friend since kindergarten, Kevin Rogers, edited this volume with delicate precision. I am profoundly grateful.

And of course, Kathy, my wife, and Emma and Seth, my children, have been my greatest inspiration. For their well-being and for the blessing that I trust this book will be to you, I am glad I asked for help.

INTRODUCTION

LIFE CRASHES HAPPEN, BUT so does resilient living. Where you find resilience, you find an individual or a family bouncing forward into new realities.

***

Bouncing forward. Froma Walsh aptly defines resilience in her book, *Strengthening Family Resilience*, as "the ability to rebound from crisis and overcome life challenges."[1] Some of us just want to bounce back. The truth is that after a significant life crash, our old realities do not exist anymore. Therefore, we bounce forward into new realities.

What exactly is a life crash? For our purposes, a life crash happens when *normal* gets upended. Often, life crashes are unexpected. The grim diagnosis is delivered, the stroke happens, the phone rings in the middle of the night, and life changes.

Sometimes life crashes occur because of poor choices. Sometimes we reap the consequences of financial meltdown, relational demolition, or other destruction of *normal,* and we know that we are to blame.

When *normal* ceases to exist (whether by random circumstance or by bad choices), we desperately need to tap into our capacity for resilience!

***

My own life was cruising along quit swimmingly until the summer of 2004. I was working as a minister for a church, and my wife was staying home with our two-year-old daughter. We basked in the good life. And it had been good for quite some time. We picnicked, vacationed, dined with friends, exercised, and enjoyed our ministry.

Two weeks after our son was born in July of 2004, however, my wife became immobilized with increasing pain. The rheumatologist confirmed that she had Dermatomyositis, a rare and debilitating autoimmune disease.

Being optimistic types, we assumed that Prednisone, other medicines, and a more healthy diet would have my wife back to normal in a few weeks, despite the doctor's warnings that there was no known cure for this disease. A few months later, my wife, who has always been a petite, charmingly kind, and clear-complexioned lady, looked at me and said, "I am losing my hair, I am growing a mustache and I have a terrible rash. I have a hump on my back, I have gained 40 pounds, I can't sleep, and I don't even know who I am when I look in the mirror. I don't look like myself and I don't feel like myself. At this point, I'm going to be manlier than you."

She could not pick our son up because of extreme muscle pain and muscle loss. To add insult to injury, she itched all of the time because of the skin portion of this disease. Thankfully, we had many friends who brought us meals for several months, and my parents made the hour and a half drive on Thursdays and Sundays to help with the children and perform other household tasks that simply were not getting done.

This life continued for much longer than we ever anticipated. It was hell.

To make matters worse, I made a series of bad decisions about a new career. Our move ultimately failed and left us in a less-than-ideal financial pinch.

With a sick mom, two preschool children, and a depressed and struggling dad, we accepted a gracious offer from my wife's parents and moved in with them for a season of accepting help. Words will always fall short of the gratitude I have for both sets of our parents and the sacrificial support they provided during our life crash.

Through our extended crisis, we experienced successful treatments and doctors who listened, but not until we had a bad taste of medicines that backfired and arrogant doctors who never heard us. We have dealt with grudges, forgiveness, denial, avoidance and depression. We have accepted responsibility to do something about our situation, both the parts that were self-inflicted and those that were not. Somewhere in the midst of almost four years of struggle, we started making better decisions…life-giving decisions:

- To forgive people who made matters worse.
- To forgive ourselves and banish unnecessary guilt.
- To reject the "victim identity."
- To face reality and deal with the truth.
- To ask for and accept help.
- To intentionally set out on a path of understanding our situation, dreaming again, planning again, and facing our recurring giants.
- To help others who are experiencing a life crash.
- And to determine to live life on the upward spiral of the resilient life.

***

My wife still has Dermatomyositis. But, we continue to do everything we can to create better health for her. Just prior to the time of this writing, she picked up our son again.

Our financial situation is better. We appreciate our

families and friends as never before. And we are even thankful for the life crash. As it turns out, God has been with us all along, and we are becoming more resilient people *because of our problems, not because of the absence of our problems.*

If I can bounce forward from a life crash, I know you can as well. (I never really had any doubt about my wife!) God created *you* with the capacity for resilience! Whether you are dealing with a life-altering health condition or caring for a loved one with a long-term illness, you are resilient! Your finest hour may just be the time that you thought was your worst. If you are dealing with the crash of your finances, relationships, or career, you will discover hope and a realistic plan for the future as you fully engage this journey book.

The principles and the process of *Resilient Life* are for you! In the pages that follow, I have given you room to personalize this resilient journey to fit your own circumstances and choices.

God believes in you, and so do I…right smack in the middle of your life crash. As I write this, I am praying that you will enter the upward spiral of the resilient life! No matter what the situation, life is a gift, and today is your day!

Facing Reality

In the middle of difficulty lies opportunity.

-Albert Einstein

***

Truth

YOU WILL KNOW THE *truth and the truth will set you free.* Jesus said that. [2] But, I would like to add some important elements. You will know the truth, the truth will hurt quite a bit, and then if you face it and do something about it, the truth will set you free.

Most of us prefer fantasy and avoidance — until those shocking moments when we must face reality. Why? It's tough. But, telling the truth about your situation is essential to becoming resilient.

***

My wife holds firmly to the practice of buying new toothbrushes for our family every three months. After several years of this, I decided to buy my own toothbrush...a fancy one.

I searched online, analyzed the fine arguments of *toothbrushery*, and spent 20 minutes in the aisle inspecting the toothbrushes up close. Finally, I purchased my new best friend and a wonderful relationship began.

Until I came home one day to find my three-year-old son sitting in my recliner with *my* toothbrush in *his* mouth! As I explained to him the reasons that this was hygienically unacceptable, my five-year-old daughter walked in and listened for a moment, then said, "Oh, did he have your toothbrush in his mouth again?"

Again?

I had to face reality. I was not the only one using my toothbrush!

Of course, now I know the truth and the truth has set me free to buy a new toothbrush along with a "toothbrush safe" for our bathroom to ensure that I do not share slobber with my son ever again!

Simply put, facing reality can be painful. Perhaps the greatest source of discomfort is in admitting that we have a problem. In families, this truth is especially difficult to accept.

Dr. Froma Walsh points out, "No family is problem-free. What distinguishes healthy families is not the absence of problems or suffering but rather their coping and problem-solving abilities." [3]

Quite naturally, coping and problem-solving often begin with a good cry.

One of the great examples of resilience in the Bible involves Nehemiah, the great rebuilder of the wall of Jerusalem. Before he led the rebuilding of the wall and the people's hopes, Nehemiah, the great leader, began his journey by sitting down and weeping.

***

> *I asked them about the Jews who had survived the captivity and about how things were going in Jerusalem. They said to me,*

"Things are not going well for those who returned to the province of Judah. They are in great trouble and disgrace. The wall of Jerusalem has been torn down, and the gates have been burned."

When I heard this, I sat down and wept.

-Nehemiah 1:2-4

***

Nehemiah asked for and received an honest evaluation of the current and bitter realities. Then, he sat down and cried.

Following this assessment and initial response, he repented, asked God for help, and began planning and working to rebuild the wall of Jerusalem. Still, he began by acknowledging the ugly truth of the situation.

***

During the first months of my wife's illness, I retreated to my work. Working as a minister at the time, I was organizing several important yearly events and allowed the success of those events to consume me. In addition, I was leading the inaugural work project of our local Habitat for Humanity affiliate, in which I served as president. While other people brought food, kept the children, and helped my wife, I made the egregious mistake of burying myself in the work of saving the world. Or, you might say, of avoiding reality.

Until one day in early September of 2004, when my wife informed me that we needed to get out of town together to evaluate our plight. Living in Tennessee at the time, we dropped the children off at my parents' house and drove to Memphis for a two-day getaway.

We cried all the way to Memphis.

That trip marked an important day on our journey through this illness. For this was the day that I faced the bitter reality that my wife had a long-term illness and that I had been avoiding it. On this day, she regained the partner that she needed for the painful journey.

***

To be a resilient person, or family, or group, you must face reality. This is the first and most important move as we enter the upward spiral of resilience.

***

She never saw it coming. She was drifting along in her tidy little life, as naïve and immortal as the next fortysomething. Suddenly both of her parents were catastrophically ill, and her life was abruptly derailed. Everything that had been familiar vanished and what was to come was terrifyingly uncertain. But as dumbfounded days turned into months, she finally told the truth. "I am not just their little girl anymore; I am the caregiver of my parents who are dying."[4]

***

He sat down to work on the bills again. The numbers seemed to be in reverse of what they should. Somehow the dream and the charmed existence of the past decade did not match up with the numbers before him. He cried and he prayed. He admitted bad choices and foolish spending. And that was the night that he finally told the truth…and was set free to rebuild.

***

Whatever the reasons, life crashes of all sorts tend to happen. But, resilience happens as well, and it begins with facing reality.

Remember Joseph, the kid with the "Amazing Technicolor Dream Coat?" He had dreams…mostly about him being the boss of all of his brothers! That wasn't so bad (I suspect we all like to dream of being more powerful than we currently are). Joseph's mistake was that he *told* his brothers about these dreams! Not surprisingly, they did not share his fondness for those visions of his greatness. To make matters worse, his father, Jacob, did what all parenting seminars do not recommend: choose your favorite child and let the other kids know.

***

> *Now Jacob loved Joseph more than any of his other children because Joseph had been born to him in his old age. So one day he gave Joseph a special gift — a beautiful robe. But his brothers hated him.*
>
> -Genesis 37:3-4

***

If you couple Jacob's partiality with the fancy coat and those irritating dreams, it's no wonder that Joseph had problems when he showed up to check on his older brothers. They contemplated killing him and only after a plea from Reuben, the oldest brother, did they settle for throwing him in a pit and then selling him to gypsies. Happens all the time, right?

Well, Joseph wound up in the house of Potiphar, who was on the personal staff of Pharaoh, the Egyptian leader. Joseph was a slave, then the head slave, until Mrs. Potiphar came onto him in a rather determined fashion and ripped his shirt off. This was the point at which Joseph faced reality — "I think she likes me."

Of course, Joseph made a wise decision and ran away only to have Mrs. Potiphar falsely accuse him of sexual crimes. So, Joseph wound up in jail and was then forgotten until finally one day he re-emerged from prison, gained favor in Pharaoh's sight, and became a very powerful national leader.

It seems to me that Joseph was pretty resilient, in part because Joseph faced some very important realities:

- My brothers hate me. In fact, they just beat me up and sold me!
- Mrs. Potiphar likes me. So much so that she just falsely accused me of a terrible crime.
- I am in prison. I have been left alone and forgotten.
- But perhaps the most important reality that Joseph faced and held onto through this whole extended life crash is this one:

***

The Lord was with Joseph and blessed him greatly as he served in the home of his Egyptian master.

-Genesis 39:2

***

The Lord was with him, making everything run smoothly and successfully.

-Genesis 39:23

***

Frankly, Joseph's life doesn't sound like "smoothly and successfully" to me! Then again, the events of Joseph's life were just painful circumstances, not death sentences. Clearly, Joseph lived through these harsh times by receiving the real presence of God in the midst of adversity.

The first and most important move into resilience is to face reality. Tell the truth about what's going on and what has happened. Then, remember the truth that God is still with you in the middle of the life crash.

***

Conflict

Playing hide-n-seek and wishing that problems would "just go away" tends to be the first response for many of us. Avoidance is a self-defense mechanism for dealing with circumstances that we are not ready to handle. However, this tactic only proves helpful for a very limited time.

"Problems do not go away. They must be worked through or else they remain, forever a barrier to the growth and development of the spirit," states M. Scott Peck in his classic work, *The Road Less Traveled.* [5] In fact, Peck even says; "It is only because of problems that we grow mentally and spiritually." [6]

Do you know of any great people who have been exempt from problems? In most cases, the way they handled and overcame difficulty is precisely what equipped them for greatness!

As you tell the truth about your circumstances, perhaps this model from the world of conflict management will prove helpful. In each situation, we find a presenting issue that is above the line. But to get to the heart of the matter, you must identify the real issue that is below the line. [7]

***

Presenting Issue

The Real Issue

For example, you may be experiencing depression and anxiety related to being diagnosed with a long-term or severe illness. This is the position or presenting issue. Yet, if you explore your most honest thoughts, you may find that below the line you are really dealing with spiritual doubt and fear, not just the external conditions of a disease or illness.

The more precise you can be in determining what you're really struggling with, the better you can begin to address your situation. With this example, you might plumb deeper by asking questions such as:

- What am I afraid of?
- Do I think that my illness means that God is not listening?
- Why would I think that God would forsake me?
- Am I living with a sense of entitlement, that I should never encounter problems?
- If other people have been faithful through the midst of difficulty, can't I?
- Who do I need to ask to help guide me through these troubled waters?

***

Responsibility

He looked dead…almost. Slumped over, disheveled, and worried, his answer confirmed my suspicions.

"How are you doing?" I asked with my greeting skills on autopilot.

"I'm circling the drain, just circling the drain," he replied in Eeyore fashion.

***

I had never heard this self-diagnosis before, but the image those words painted in my mind coupled with the man before me were crystal clear. This man seemed to have given up, or to have given in to the opposite of the resilient life. He had adopted the victim mentality, as if there were nothing he could do.

A victim mentality stands in direct opposition to responsibility and hope. True, you probably did not ask for your difficult circumstances, and in some cases you may have had very little to do with it at all. But whether your current reality is a product of poor choices or a product of circumstances beyond your control, you must take complete responsibility for today.

It is what it is. Now, what are you going to do?

"To be free people, we must assume total responsibility for ourselves, but in doing so must possess the capacity to reject responsibility that is not truly ours," says M. Scott Peck. [8] In other words, decide what is within your power to do something about and what is not. Then, take complete responsibility for doing whatever you can do to add life to your situation.

***

In this final section of the chapter, I encourage you to work through each question and exercise with full honesty, telling the truth, facing reality, confronting the pain, and taking responsibility for your life from this point forward. After assessing your reality, I will join you again in the next chapter to help you learn how to better interpret and understand your situation in order to become the resilient person that God created you to be!

Discovering Your Current Reality

1. What is the truth of your current condition?

2. What are you doing or not doing that is perpetuating the problem?

3. What are you doing or have ceased doing that is creating good in your life?

Understanding Your System

Human beings, like plants, grow in the soil of acceptance, not in the atmosphere of rejection.
-John Powell

***

Understanding Yourself

YOU ARE UNIQUE! NO other person will ever have the same beauty, quirks, or contribution to life that you have right now in the way that only you can do. Your tone of voice, sense of humor, distinct smell, peculiar walk, and loves are specific to you. And no one but you can turn your problems into a story that inspires others to overcome their own problems!

That being said, you may also find it helpful to learn about the ways in which you are similar to other people. We usually refer to these as personality types. Over the years, I have found personality assessment tools to be extremely insightful, often leading to an "aha" moment. As a caveat however, you should not accept any evaluation of your personality to be a crutch or a life sentence. So, learn and use what you discover to better your self-awareness.

Why is this important? Understanding yourself and your system will shine crucial light on your life crash situation.

In the resource section at the end of the book, you will find several good sources for becoming more self-aware. But for our purposes at the moment, you may find Dr. Gary Smalley and Dr. John Trent's personality instrument to be very valuable. While this assessment may not be as technical or extensive as others, I find this brief self-diagnosis to be quite helpful.

To fully engage this quick assessment, go through each section and circle the words or phrases that sound like you. When you are done, add the number of circled phrases, double that number, and write the number in the space provided. Then you will be ready to chart your personality strengths. [9]

Lion		Beaver	
Likes authority Confident Firm Enjoys challenges Problem solver Bold Goal-driven Strong-willed Self-reliant Persistent	Takes charge Determined Enterprising Competitive Productive Purposeful Adventurous Independent Controlling Action-oriented	Enjoys instructions Consistent Reserved Practical Factual Perfectionistic Detailed Inquisitive Persistent Sensitive	Accurate Controlled Predictable Orderly Conscientious Discerning Analytical Precise Scheduled Deliberate
"Let's do it now!" Double the number chosen:____		"How was it done in the past?" Double the number chosen:____	
Otter		**Golden Retriever**	
Enthusiastic Visionary Energetic Promoter Mixes easily Fun-loving Spontaneous Creative-new ideas Optimistic Infectious laughter	Takes Risks Motivator Very verbal Friendly Enjoys popularity Likes variety Enjoys change Group-oriented Initiator Inspirational	Sensitive feelings Calm Non-demanding Avoids confrontations Enjoys routine Warm and relational Adaptable Thoughtful Patient Good listener	Loyal Even-keeled Gives in Indecisive Dislikes change Dry humor Sympathetic Nurturing Tolerant Peace maker
"Trust me! It'll work out!" Double the number chosen:____		"Let's keep things the way they are." Double the number chosen:____	

Graph your score on this chart:

Personality Strengths Chart

	Lion	Beaver	Otter	Golden Retriever
40				
30				
20				
10				
0				

Essentially, as Smalley describes, we find these personality types in the fourth grade classroom. When the teacher asks the class to turn a lump of clay into a face, the lion is done in 45 seconds. The otter seeks to involve everyone and quickly has someone making a nose and someone else making ears. The golden retriever reminds the otter not to leave out or offend any of the kids. And when the class has finished their creations and the teacher asks them to put up their clay, the beaver cries out, "I'm still working on the lower eyelashes!"[10]

Lion. If you are a lion, you like action. You are decisive, bold, and often in charge. And you wouldn't have it any other way. Patience may be a growth area for you!

Beaver. If you scored high in the beaver area, you are detail-oriented and probably prefer to spend the majority of your time working alone on tasks, and not so much with people. Spotlights cause you to break out in hives.

Otter. You are a people person. You will typically be the life of the party, a great connector, and spontaneous. This drives some people crazy, and you could probably stand a bit more attention to the details.

Golden Retriever. If you scored high in this area, you are sensitive to the needs of others. You may find yourself being the caregiver for a loved one. You are a peacemaker. When the lions and the otters battle it out, you go home and worry all night, while they sleep just fine.

***

Understanding yourself and what makes you tick is an essential step to the resilient life, especially in a life crash situation. If you would like a more detailed personality assessment, I recommend checking one of the links in the resource section of this book.

***

Your Crazy Family

Understanding creates awareness, and awareness should help you become a more gracious human being.

But, you still may think that your in-laws are nuts.

That's fine. They probably are. So are you. So am I. Get over it. You will not be changing anyone in the near future (or in the distant future for that matter). You can really only change yourself, which is a tough enough job.

Joseph (in the biblical story in Genesis) found himself in a family system that most psychologists would not recommend. Fraught with favorite sons and special treatment and excessive sibling rivalry, their example was less than stellar. If you were to do a family genogram with Joseph, you would find a few problems in his family history. Jacob did not get along with his brother Esau, nor was their mother, Rebekah, much help in the peace between those two brothers. You see where this is going.

Nevertheless, their family genogram does not only reveal faults. It also reveals great models of faith and love. I'm thinking of Joseph's great-granddad, Abraham. He made some major mistakes, but he also serves as one of the greatest examples of faith. After being tricked into marrying the older sister of his beloved, Jacob worked an extra seven years to prove his love for Rachel.

So like most systems, theirs was a mix of bitter rivalry and dirty tricks, great faith and uncommon love.

More understanding helps us to become more gracious. In a family crash, it helps to understand that what we do as individuals affects the whole. When mom gets sick, things change and it affects the whole family. We do well to understand that as we make changes and propose and explore changes as a group, that not all of us make these transitions at the same pace. Some of us have moved on to new realities, and others of us aren't sure what happened. Some of us engage in conflictive discussions quite readily and go home and sleep fine, while others of us stay up all night worrying about the ones who differed so sharply, and some of us avoid these conflicts at all costs.

To better understand your own family system, I suggest that you first gain a better understanding of family systems theory and principles. So, what does "family systems theory" mean? Basically, the idea is that families are not merely a collection of individuals but a living and developing system whose members are essentially interconnected. The ways that we communicate, handle conflict, talk about each other, and live together have a tremendous impact on how well we will survive our life crash. The family system always has the capacity to become healthy and well-balanced or sick and harmful to its members. Check out this web page to gain more insight into family systems theory:
www.thebowencenter.org

What, you may be asking, is the point of all of this? The purpose of understanding your own personality and the dynamics of your family is to become more self-aware and thus, more gracious to the people in your system. If you are experiencing the stress of long-term illness, financial meltdown, or a similar life crash, this understanding will help you manage significant stressors more mercifully.

***

Your Resilient Family

One way to begin exploring your own family's resilience is by doing a family genogram. I would suggest tracing your family back for at least three or four generations. As you think of your parents, grandparents, great-grandparents, and other relatives, ask two questions:

1. What difficulties and problems did they encounter in their lives? (Think of business failures, the Depression, illnesses, untimely deaths, bad choices, etc.)
2. How did they survive or overcome? Did they ever overcome? If not, why not? If so, how so?

In this process, you will discover stories of disappointment and stories in which to take great pride.

Learn from both. It is important that you uncover and examine these triumphs and failures from your past and from your family's past. By identifying how they learned to cope and live again, you may learn to transfer those lessons into your current circumstances. You may wish to follow the example format below. I would suggest selecting one or two individuals from each generation.

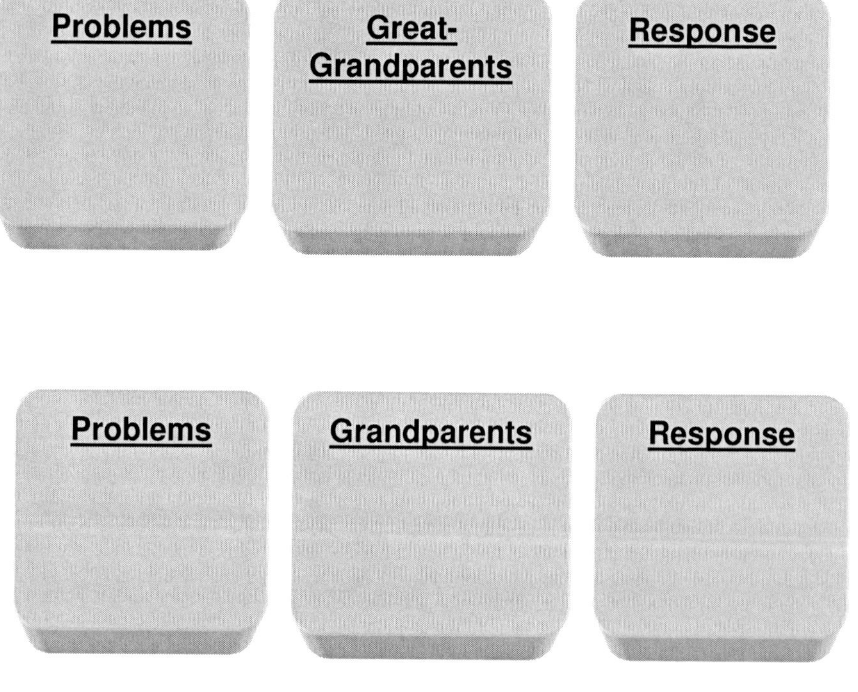

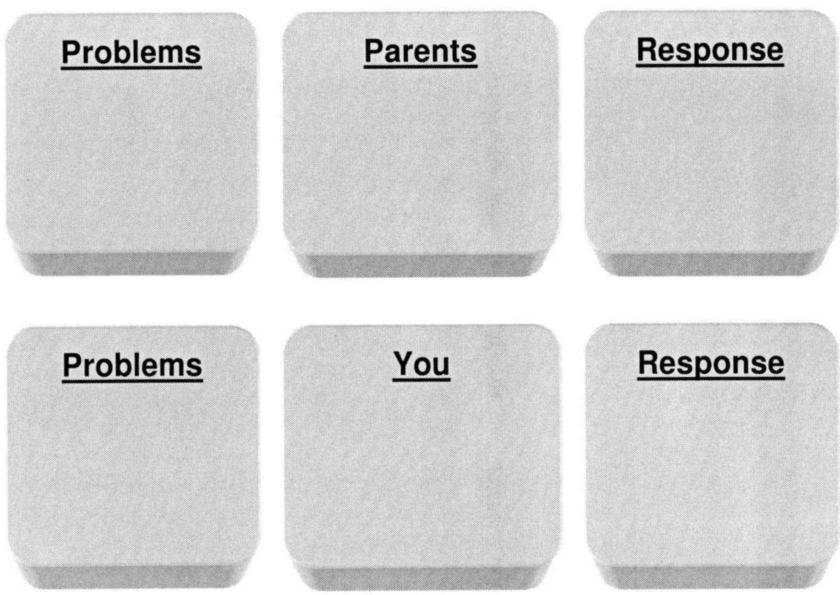

Hopefully, this exercise has opened your eyes to the way that your family has overcome and dealt with adversity. Perhaps you're seeing a trait of resilience.

But what if you discovered a lack of resilience? What if you discovered a "victim mentality" that has been passed down from generation to generation? As you will learn in chapter five, everyone has the capacity for resilience. This means that you can learn resilience and begin a new family tradition! If this exercise has exposed problems, at least you have faced reality. Now, you can continue the process of the resilient life and learn to face that giant!

***

Don't Say The "C" Word: *Change*

Change and transition have a significant impact upon your family or group. As your group experiences a move, a change in leadership, a financial transition, or any type of adjustment, you will have tension. Why? Because not everyone in the family or group transitions at the same speed.

In our early years of marriage, my wife and I moved numerous times from Oklahoma to Arkansas back to Oklahoma to Texas to Tennessee to Missouri and back to Oklahoma once again all in the span of 12 years. As we approached a move, I typically spent the six months prior to the move in heavy preparation and then hit the ground running at our new destination. On the other hand, my wife spent the first six months at our new location in a high degree of disorientation and grief. We simply transitioned in different ways and at different speeds.

William Bridges, in his seminal work, *Transitions*, describes three stages of a transition: ending, the neutral zone, and making a new beginning. [11] This model may best describe his theory:

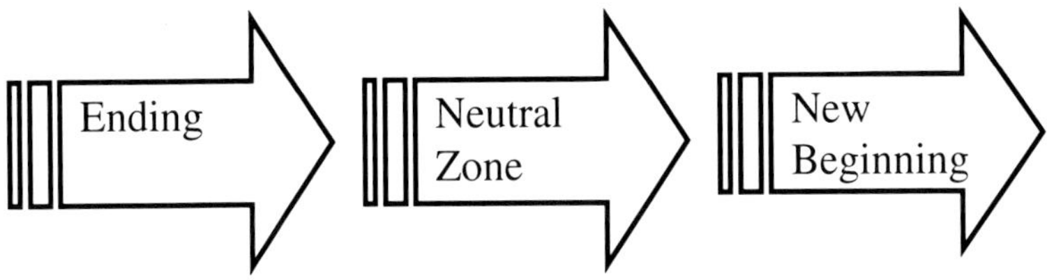

You and your loved one are living somewhere in this process. But as with most areas of life, we are also unique in the way we transition. We don't all transition at the same pace or with the same expectations.

Every transition begins with an ending. Something is lost; something has changed; something has ended. That *something* may be freedom on the part of the caregiver and the patient, or it could be financial or relational ease.

Next, we experience the neutral zone. This is a place

of disorientation, disenchantment, and discomfort. Nothing seems to make sense. Your world has been turned upside down, and you have not gotten your bearings.

Finally, you make a new beginning. At this stage, you adopt a new routine, a new normal. In the case of a long-term illness, however, the caregiver and care recipient rarely make the transition at the same speed. While the patient comes to terms with his or her illness and even his or her impending death, the loved one refuses to admit it, or vice versa.

Perhaps you should take a moment to reflect on the dynamics of a transition. Where are you? Where are your loved ones in this current transition?

***

Fighting Fair

Conflict is not inherently bad. *How* we handle conflict can be bad.

Inevitably, where you find a group of two or three people, you will eventually find conflict. Why? Individuals have different interpretation systems and worldviews. Therefore, on a regular basis, we disagree, especially in the pressure-cooked situation of a life crash.

As we disagree, we discover that people have unique conflict styles. In conflicts, you will often find people who predominantly tend to:

- Persuade
- Compel
- Avoid or accommodate
- Collaborate
- Negotiate
- Support

***

For instance, if you tend to avoid conflict and someone else in your system has a style of compelling, which is often very heavy-handed, you may feel bullied. This, in turn, will lead to resentment. Likewise, it is quite difficult to negotiate with someone who only wishes to persuade you of his or her position.

***

I suggest these basic reminders when dealing with conflict:

- Initiate the conversation. Ignoring the problem will only cause it to fester.
- Establish ground rules of civility, i.e. no name calling or yelling.
- Identify the problem. Allow each party to describe the problem as they see it.
- Focus on the *what* — not the *who*.
- Generate possible solutions.
- Either agree to one of these solutions or agree to differ.

***

What is your conflict style? How does conflict normally play out in your system of family or friends? One helpful tool is *Discover Your Conflict Management Style* by Speed Leas. You can learn more about these tools by checking the resource section in this book.

***

From Grief to Hope

If you are in the middle of a life crash, you are also grieving. Grief is natural and often disorienting.

Even if you are not experiencing the loss of a loved one, you may be experiencing the loss of freedom, health, financial well being, or a relationship. All of these situations can lead to grief.

So, what should you expect when you grieve? Granger Westberg describes 10 common encounters when grieving:[12]

- Shock
- High emotion
- Depression or loneliness
- Physical symptoms of distress
- Panic
- Guilt
- Anger and resentment
- Resistance to a return to normal
- Hope

- New Reality

***

You may not experience all of these. Yet, each of these is normal. Shock, high emotion, depression, physical symptoms of distress, panic, guilt, anger, resentment, and resistance are all normal, but only helpful for a limited time. If you find yourself stuck in any of these areas, you may need to ask a friend, minister, or counselor for help in moving forward again.

Each person's grief is unique; therefore, no timeline can be set to fit everyone. However, God does not intend for you to spend the rest of your life feeling guilty and angry. This would not be good for you or for anyone else.

Eventually, you should expect to embrace hope and a new reality! While this may seem unrealistic currently, as you begin to enter the upward spiral of resilience, you will come to a new and brighter reality once again. This, too, is natural and to be expected.

***

Becoming resilient and facing reality is wrapped up in understanding what's going on in your system…whether that is family, a group of friends, coworkers, or church members. Once you have processed this information and perhaps experienced an "aha" moment about yourself or your loved ones, you will be even further grounded in reality and ready to dream again!

Discovering Your System

1. What is the most significant finding you have made in this chapter about yourself or your family?

2. How will this awareness change your perception of your next group encounter?

3. Which resource do you need to explore to gain a better understanding of your system? Do you need to talk with a counselor, minister, friend, or coach?

Dreaming Again

Commit your work to the Lord, and then your plans will succeed.

-Proverbs 16:3

***

Dreaming God-sized Dreams

WE ALL DREAM DREAMS. Sometimes we hold onto a dream for years. When life crashes, however, we often let go of our dreams. Or worse yet, we settle for a life with small dreams or none at all.

When Jesus died, his followers weren't quite sure what the future held. They were in the neutral zone. Then, on a momentous day for those early disciples, Peter quoted the powerful words of the prophet Joel:

***

> *In the last days, God said, I will pour out my Spirit upon all people. Your sons and daughters will prophesy, your young men will see visions, and your old men will dream dreams.*
>
> -Acts 2:17

We tend to think that dreaming is for the kids. But in this call to a new vision, the old ones are supposed to dream. In the context of this momentous day, it is difficult to imagine those dreams being ones of ease and personal indulgence. Surely, these older people dreamt of something much greater than themselves.

We can also learn a lot about dreams from Joseph. He dreamed those dreams that his brothers hated. He interpreted dreams in prison for the cupbearer and the chief baker (evidently, Pharaoh had a very upset stomach). Then, he interpreted visions for Pharaoh, which soon turned into concrete plans to survive the famine.

> *One night the cupbearer and the baker each had a dream, and each dream had its own meaning. The next morning Joseph noticed the dejected look on their faces. "Why do you look so worried today?" He asked. And they replied, "We both had dreams last night, but there is no one here to tell us what they mean." "Interpreting dreams is God's business," Joseph replied. "Tell me what you saw."*
>
> -Genesis 40:5-8

***

Notice this crucial element. Joseph *begins* by linking the interpretation of those dreams to God. In these two instances, we learn that both the giving and the interpreting of dreams thrived with God's involvement, which inherently made the dreams bigger than any one person.

And this gets us well on our way to the point. ***As we dream again, we must dream God-sized dreams, not me-sized dreams!***

As an individual, could you dream and pray that God would make you what he has created you to be? What if you traded all the worry and the angst of "who am I" and "what is my place" with this prayer, "God, make me what you have created me to be." That's a big dream!

As a family, could you trust God with the dream of what you want your family to look like? Would you trust God enough to just give him your dream, knowing that you might not get it back looking quite the same as you originally envisioned?

Perhaps you have an even larger question. Do you believe that a dream is still possible, given your current situation? If not, you need to determine precisely what is standing in the way. Most likely, the inability to dream again is rooted in your view of God and yourself. Many people experience severe limitations to their dreams because of misguided views of God and themselves.

***

Your View of God

Froma Walsh identifies three keys to the belief system of resilient people. First, she notes that resilient people and families make meaning out of adversity. Then, she points out that resilient people generate a positive outlook by believing in spiritual realities that transcend circumstances.[13]

This sense of meaning and hope eludes many people because of a major roadblock of which they are largely unaware. For too many individuals, their view of God is that of a despotic, angry, manipulative being. Granted, not many folks would admit to such a thing or perhaps even be able to articulate the roadblock as such. But in countless conversations with people who are stuck, I find that this is the root of the problem.

A recent study of "The Values and Beliefs of the American Public" shed significant light on the way Americans view God. For 31.4 percent of Americans, God is authoritarian, deeply involved in the world and basically angry about what he sees. About 23 percent of the people view God as more grieved over the state of humans and believe in a Benevolent God. A third group of some 16 percent sees a Critical God, but expects very little divine wrath or help. And the final group of 24.4 percent holds to a view of the Distant God who is sitting back to see what happens with us.[14]

Predominantly, these views of God sound more problematic than helpful. Could it be that there is a better way of viewing and understanding God?

What if God, the Source of Life, is more like the *perfect father*? Not abusive, or overbearing. Not a pushover or a control freak. What if God is for you? What if God is rooting for you, and even giving you what you need to be a mature and loving human being? Could it be that God is granting love, joy, peace, patience, kindness, goodness, gentleness, faithfulness, and self-control (yes, even self-control) in unlimited abundance regardless of our circumstances? Could it be that the real problem is our receiving the gift? [15]

***

Your View of Yourself

If you could possibly accept this view of God and deeply internalize it, you would then gain a truer picture of yourself. Throughout history, men have grappled with the question of anthropology, which in theological terms has to do with whether people are inherently good or evil.

While such a consideration may seem irrelevant, I assure you it is crucial. I have met far too many people who were convinced that God was mean, they were incurably bad, and God was punishing them with a miserable life. I have also met too many people who thumbed their nose at

God and esteemed themselves too highly, thinking that they were somehow entitled to a life with no problems.

Clearly, we experience and choose both good and evil in our lives. We just need a vision of God and ourselves with which we can live and die. I like this explanation given by Thomas Merton, a Trappist monk, who lived during the 20th century:

***

> *The soul of man, left to its own natural level, is a potentially lucid crystal left in darkness. It is perfect in its own nature, but it lacks something that it can only receive from outside and above itself. But when the light shines in it, it becomes in a manner transformed into light and seems to lose its nature in the splendor of a higher nature, the nature of the light that is in it.*
>
> -Thomas Merton [16]

***

Essentially, Merton explains that God has created you well. But, you desperately need the Source of Light. And God wants you to receive that transcendent light. With this view of God and yourself, a dream doesn't seem out of the question. In fact, you are free to dream God-sized dreams.

***

Free to Dream

Have you ever known the truth about your situation, but just couldn't grasp it until someone asked you a direct question? Perhaps the following story will serve as a provocative nudge to embrace your dream.

Bruce Wilkinson tells the story of debating with another man at a restaurant about whether or not everyone could really pursue a dream. He was almost at the point of giving up when their waitress Sonja approached.

***

I asked her, "Are you doing what you've always wished you could be doing?"

She looked at me questioningly. "What do you mean?" she asked.

I said, "Well, I mean maybe you *are* doing your dream, and that would be terrific. But I wonder, do you have a Big Dream inside of your heart that hasn't come true yet?"

Sonja thought for a moment. Then she said, "My mother is a nurse. My sister is a nurse. I always dreamed of becoming a nurse."

"Would you have been a good nurse?" I asked.

Sonja became emotional. "I would have been a really good nurse," she said softly.

"Would you like to be a nurse at this very moment?" I asked.

"Yes," she said.

So I took another risk. "Do you happen to believe that God wants you to be a nurse?" I asked.

She looked away for a minute, then said, "I think so."

"If God wants you to be a nurse, then there must be a way for you to be one," I said. "What has stopped you?"

Sonja listed the reasons: an education cut short by marriage, then two children, then the demands of raising a family. "Now it's impossible," she said. "It's too late." I heard the sadness in her voice.

"What would have to happen for you to become a nurse?" I asked.

"We don't have enough money," she said. "I can't afford a baby sitter, so I can't go to school."

"So, if you had a baby sitter, you would go to school?" I asked.

"Yes," she said without hesitation.

I glanced at my producer friend to make sure he was taking this all in. Then I took another risk. "Sonja, I believe there's somebody in your life who cares about you and would baby sit your children for free. Who is that person?"

Sonja thought for a moment, and then her face lit up. "It's my mother!" she exclaimed. "She just retired two months ago! She loves her grandchildren. And she's always wanted me to have my dream. She'd baby sit my kids for free if I just asked her!"

While she spoke, her eyes brimmed with tears. Mine did, too. Anytime I see someone else's dream surfacing, I'm deeply touched, because I know how sad it is not to be able to live your dream.

Without even taking our order, Sonja slid in next to a friend at another table to announce that she was going back to school. "I'm going to be a nurse!" she said with tears of joy.

My friend sat across from me, shaking his head. "If I hadn't seen it with my own eyes," he said, "I wouldn't have believed it. Maybe you're right. Maybe everybody *does* have a Big Dream."[17]

***

There's a God-sized dream! Helping other people realize their own dreams.

In your current situation, you should be free to dream! God wants good for you! You *need* good for you, no matter what your circumstances! God specializes in delivering people from life crashes. So, pray for a God-sized dream. Ask for the self-control and passion to pursue the dream, to do your part. Then, give that dream to God. You can trust God with it.

***

Entitlement vs. Gift

What about your circumstances? Must everything be perfect in order for everything to be perfect?

There exists a crucial distinction between viewing life with a sense of entitlement and viewing life as a gift. The person who approaches life with a sense of entitlement expects to experience no sickness and no problems. When life crashes do happen, these people are bitter, angry, and miserable. They blame everyone, including God, the doctors, the other person, or themselves.

On the other hand, people who see life as a gift tend to be more grateful. Even in bad circumstances, these people find a way to be appreciative. Not that they enjoy difficult circumstances, but these people seem to find life even in the valley of the shadow of death.

***

At age 31, I slammed into a brick wall on the interstate of my life. My wife became terribly ill. About two miserable years later, I realized that I was living with a sense of entitlement. I didn't think we should have to deal with significant illness at our age. This kind of thing wasn't supposed to happen until we were much older! Consequently, I became angry, bitter, and miserable.

Then, I began to reassess our reality. Had God abandoned us? No. In fact, God had surrounded us with hundreds of friends and family members who helped us far more than we would have ever asked. Were our dreams vanquished? No. Adjusted, but not vanquished.

My wife and I have always dreamt of developing books and seminars to inspire and help guide families into harmony with God. We have consistently desired to help other people. Now, we actually know what we're talking about! And we have an increasing amount of opportunities to bless other people's lives.

In some unexpected ways, we are better people *because of* our struggles, not because of the absence of those struggles! God is taking our small dreams and turning them into God-sized dreams right smack dab in the middle of difficult circumstances! Our lives have pain, and yet we are still living the dream! What a gift! As it turns out, everything does not need to be perfect, to live your God-sized dream.

***

From Here to There

You are here now. And yes, after facing reality and understanding your system, you can and must dream again!

From the reality of your life at this moment, you can begin to dream a God-sized dream. If that thought gives you a jolt, I recommend engaging fully in the exercise below to help you chart your course from *here* to *there.*

In the left column, write the truth of your "here" situation. In the right column, draft your dream…your "there." In the next chapter, we will work on developing the "how" of the middle column.

HERE	THERE
1.	**1.**
2.	**2.**
3.	**3.**
4.	**4.**

Discovering Your God-Sized Dreams

1. Do you think God is for or against you? Why?

2. Ask, believe, and receive. Carve out 15 minutes to meditate on these three words. Is some limiting belief getting in the way of your dreams? How can you transform that limiting belief?

3. How will good come from your adversity?

4. Is it possible that God could help you transcend your current circumstances?

5. What is your God-sized dream?

Planning Again

Spectacular achievement is always preceded by unspectacular preparation.

-Robert Schuller

***

Plotting Your Course

In Lewis Carroll's beloved classic *Alice in Wonderland*, the following scene unfolds as Alice asks the Cheshire Cat for directions.

***

"Would you tell me, please, which way I ought to go from here?'"

"That depends a good deal on where you want to get to," said the Cat.

"I don't much care where —" said Alice.

"Then it doesn't matter which way you go," said the Cat.

"— so long as I get *somewhere*," Alice added as an explanation.

"Oh, you're sure to do that," said the Cat, "if you only walk long enough." [18]

***

How do you get from here to there? If your "here" is not grounded in reality, you will have immense difficulty in defining your "there." Alice had very little sense of "here" and almost no sense of "there." If you don't know where you're headed, you could end up anywhere.

The answer to direction has everything to do with intentionality. Purposefully assessing reality and charting your course will provide a sense of peace in troubled times.

Planning may not sound as alluring as dreaming. But don't be fooled. Planning and developing a strategy should be just as inspired as the dream. God does not abandon you at the end of the dream. God will be with you as you plan action steps, think wisely, and chart your course.

To create your strategy for living the dream, begin with the end in mind and work backwards to here and now. If your goal is to be debt-free with significant savings in five years, you will need to break that goal down. You must determine what steps will be necessary for you to move consistently toward your goal. Perhaps you will need to talk to a financial advisor, take a class, or find an accountability partner. Reaching this noble goal will likely mean opening an account and saving a certain amount per month. Assessing past realities, you may need to develop a better budgeting system or create a debt snowball plan. Think backwards from the goal to develop your strategy in small, incremental steps.

What your life will look like five years from today depends on what you do in the next 24 hours. This does *not* mean you have to do it all in the next 24 hours. What this provocative statement *does* mean is that you must begin taking small steps today! Most people who have experienced significant success in any area of life will tell you that success does not normally happen by great leaps and bounds. Rather, success happens by taking one right step after another. And occasionally, you will experience a great leap in the midst of those many small steps. If you take the actions that you can reasonably take today, you will begin to experience small victories immediately. Think about this as you complete this chapter, then stop to fully engage the growth exercises.

***

Balance

As you develop a God-sized plan for living your God-sized dream, you must remember to remain balanced. A healthy plan of action will not be lopsided, but rather well-rounded. Please consider spirituality, vibrant health, strong relationships, adventure, work, service, and financial strength as you develop a plan. Perhaps these questions will help sharpen your thought process.

Five years from today, where do you want to be spiritually? Where does God want you to be? If you are spiritually depleted at that time, you will have engaged in an adventure in missing the point. [19] Don't. Decide what you will do daily, weekly, monthly, and yearly to posture yourself to receive God's abundance of peace, clarity, and love. How will you build the foundation of your dream with prayer, meditation, contemplation, fasting, spiritual walks, spiritual retreats, or days of prayer placed in your plan?

Where do you want to be physically? Could you be in better shape five years from today than you are today? Will you trade a heavy, greasy, indulgent diet for a fresh, green, clean, energizing diet? Could you carve out 15 to 30 minutes every single day for creative exercise routines? Will you turn off late-night television and rest adequately? Perhaps you are dealing with a major illness and are more limited in this area. What small steps can you take?

What about the people you love? In five years, wouldn't it be great to be dating your spouse and engaging in special adventures and dates with your kids or parents? What if you were having a weekly breakfast with a friend or a group of friends? What if your loved one is not here in five years? What if you aren't? You know what's important. Plan your days accordingly and create moments for the people you love.

Five years from now, what do you want to be exploring? You have mountains to climb, gardens to plant, games to play, places to see, performances to enjoy! Even if you are currently limited financially and in terms of mobility, intentionally create and find ways to explore. If nothing else, check out music from the library and learn to enjoy and listen deeply to the classics. Plan to explore God's wonderful world of nature, sport, travel, and the arts.

What contribution will you have made to God's mission in the world? Who will you help and how? How does your job make the world a better place? How can you do your job to make the world a better place? Who needs your encouragement? What one life could you influence with hope or practical help? Plan it and give it!

If you are reading this book, you may likely be financially strapped. If this is so, you are not resigned to a life of debt and financial uncertainty. There is a way.

In the middle of my wife's prolonged illness, I made a poor choice in changing careers and incurred significant additional credit card debt in a fairly short amount of time. I was unable to pay the debt (struggling even to meet the minimum payments due), and eventually moved in with my in-laws because of my wife's health problems and because of the financial disaster I had created. Even after we moved in with them, I struggled to make enough money to meet all of our obligations. This was the most embarrassing and humiliating season of my life.

I finally began to develop a strategy and create a future of financial freedom. Part of my plan involved asking for and accepting help. Sounds like face reality, huh? I also seriously curbed my spending and began creating additional income. I also knew that God wanted me to make better choices, to be a better steward, to ask for help, and to work hard. I did, and soon, we were making small steps toward a positive financial situation.

What are your goals for financial well-being in five years? How will you get there? What is the truth you need to tell? Who might you need to ask for help?

***

Faithfulness

After the dream and the plan and the strategy, you must get to work. Essentially, planning is about discipline and self-control, which are fruit of the Spirit, given by God. You have the capacity for self-control.

To be sure, discipline also leads to greater freedom. The more often you do the right things that you don't necessarily feel like doing, the more likely you are to experience freedom.

To live your dream, you must practice what Eugene Peterson calls "a long obedience in the same direction." [20] Step by step, day by day, you will begin to see improvements as you enter the upward spiral of the resilient life! God is with you as you plan again and do the little things every day. Before you face your giants, you need to build on your dream and develop your God-sized plan for the life God created you for!

Developing Your Strategy

1. Decide what one thing you can do on a regular basis (either daily, weekly, or monthly) to experience well-being in each of these areas:

    Spiritual:

    Physical:

    Family/Relationships:

    Personal Adventure and Development:

    Social/Service:

    Financial:

    Career/Work:

2. Work backwards from your God-sized dream (chapter 3) to create a God-sized plan in three phases.

   My God-sized Dream:

   Phase 3 Plans:

   Phase 2 Plans:

   Phase 1 Plans:

Profile in Resilience: Marcy Gardenhire
The F.A.S.T. Track to Resiliency

When the doctor told me the tumor in my lung was malignant, I said something inane, like, "You mean I have cancer? Right now, right here?" I went straight to La La Land. Two years later, the cancer is still growing and I'm still learning how to live this new life of CAT scans, chemotherapy and large doses of care and compassion. This is what has kept me going so far:

***

Faith. By far, this is the best place to start. *Have faith* is not enough. *Live faith* is better advice. I'm trying to live a faith that reminds me of a valuable truth. Even in the midst of my darkness, there is Light that shines (very dimly on some days) to erase the scary shadows lurking to trap me in hopelessness. I must be on the lookout for the Light so as not to miss the shine. It might come in the form of a neighbor who offers to mow the lawn, or the man at the grocery store who saw my bald head, asked if I was taking chemotherapy, gave me his card and said he would pray for me. These are signs of Light in our darkness. I believe this is the way God cares for us in the midst of the crap that life can bring. *God with skin on* comes to gift us with the resiliency we need for the journey and to remind us that we are not alone. Faith allows me to practice "holding lightly." This spiritual discipline invites us to take in all that is around us, all that brings joy, meaning to our lives, but hold it lightly, always willing to let go of whatever begins to control us, whatever we think we can't do without, even if that 'thing' is our life. Holding lightly is about freedom. And freedom of spirit fosters resiliency.

***

Action. A lot of feelings swirl inside when hardship hits our lives. The most toxic, I believe, is helplessness. It can paralyze us and make us forget the resources we have to confront the darkness. Taking action is one way to give helplessness the one-two punch. *Do something that puts You in charge!* Get a second opinion, join a support group, find a therapist, call the family together for a "plan of action" meeting. In the face of my 'terminal' diagnosis, I continue to plan trips for the future. I just sent in a hefty deposit for condos for next summer's family vacation. I acknowledge the gravity of my diagnosis, but I also know I have power to influence the outcome. Setting goals is an action step that empowers me.

***

Sense of Humor. Granted, there is nothing funny about Stage 4 adenocarcinoma of the lung. I feel creepy just typing those words. There is, however, room and need for humor in the resiliency resource pack. Humor goes a long way toward creating the freedom of spirit I mentioned earlier. You set the tone for how others react to your situation. If you make it the *elephant in the room* that no one mentions but everyone keeps tripping over, friends and family will scatter, bruised and battered. Don't be afraid to treat your situation with irreverence. Don't give it more power than it deserves. One of my favorite ploys is to use the "C Card" to my advantage. "Honey, would you get me another glass of tea? I'd do it myself, but, you know, I have cancer". My pastor asked how I was doing and without thinking I replied that if Mary could birth the son of Man, surely I could manage a few little tumors. At first he was startled, but then we both laughed till tears were streaming. Laughing and crying…both good for the soul!

***

Thankfulness. Yeah, right…let's all be thankful that our worst nightmare is coming true, our life is crumbling at its foundation, and we've changed our name to Job. That was my reaction when my "healing with cancer" meditation told me to thank the cancer for the things it was teaching me. But over time I've come to believe that adopting an attitude of gratitude is what enables me to accept what's happening and recognize the signs of hope and love tucked away in the shadows of this tragedy. I will never say this cancer is a gift, but many gifts have come my way because of this life crisis. I'm learning to truly live in the moment, to be more mindful of all that surrounds me in the beauty and grace that comes my way each day. Old resentments and harsh expectations of others and myself are melting away. There's no time or energy for holding on to such toxic thoughts and feelings. I am grateful for each day I feel "normal" again, each day there's no pain. Because of this disease, I'm living each day as a gift, with deep gratitude for the flashes of joy and contentment it brings. I want to focus on what I'm being given and not what I'm losing. Thank you, cancer, for the things you're teaching me.

***

Marcy Gardenhire has blessed many people through her work with AIDS patients, and more recently with the Alzheimer's Association. She has personally cared for two loved ones with Alzheimer's. Marcy and I partnered together to bring hope and timely information to family caregivers through the Caregiver Fundamentals Seminars. Simply put, she is an inspiration to me...a true example of resilience.

***

If you would like to encourage Marcy or send a donation to help with the costs of her treatment, you may contact her at marcy417@msn.com.

Facing Your Giants

The entire world is full of suffering; it is also full of overcoming it.

-Helen Keller

***

Those Recurring Giants

JUST ABOUT THE TIME you get really excited about your dreams and your plans, some giant will pop his head out. Even if the dream is God-sized and not just me-sized, and especially if the planning is wise and godly, those recurring giants will raise their ugly heads.

Becoming resilient does not exempt you from facing more giants. It equips you to face those giants with great faith!

David had already taken on bears and lions, so he was well-prepared for Goliath. Even as he experienced a life of ups and downs, many because of his own poor choices, David continued to bounce forward and face new giants.

By the time Joseph had been beaten up and sold, falsely accused of sexual crimes, thrown in and forgotten in prison, and by the time he had learned that God was with him all along, he was resilient. He had faced some rather daunting giants, and he was ready to lead a nation through seven years of famine.

Most of us have been better-groomed for resilience than we may have thought. And for those of us who think we haven't, there is still reason for hope. Did you know that new and surprising research tells us we can learn resilience at any point in life, even if we have failed to be resilient in the past? [21] Sounds like the good news of second chances to me!

Of course, just about the time we think we've made it, another giant approaches. Not because God has it in for us, but because living in a God-sized dream involves entering a God-sized battle. Things just aren't always the way they're supposed to be. And our dreams, when we give them to God, will have something to do with working to make things the way they're supposed to be once again. So we dream and we plan and then…

The giant of fear raises its head. Or, the giant of "I don't think I could ever forgive her," or the giant of "there's not enough money." Nevertheless, God is abundant in all things. The Source of Life is not running short on cash, or peace, or courage!

Inevitably in this grand process, we will face some recurring giants and some new giants that we've never smelled before. God specializes in the impossible, so that fears turn into faith, and somewhere in this process of dreaming and planning and facing giants, God also refines us and turns us into a resilient people with a God-sized dream.

***

Naming Your Giant

Fear. For many people, their giant is simply fear. Fear of doing anything different. Fear of change. Fear of failure. Fear of success. Stifled by this fear, too many people become stagnant and settle for less.

What are you afraid of? Is it the dream itself? Do you fear coming clean? Becoming vulnerable? Do you fear an unanswered prayer?

These are all legitimate fears. But each one represents a giant that stands in your way. In order to enter the upward spiral of the resilient life, you must name your fear and face it. Though it may seem overwhelming from your perspective, this giant is no match for God.

***

I command you — be strong and courageous! Do not be afraid or discouraged. For the Lord your God is with you wherever you go.

Joshua 1:9

***

Pray to know what you must do to face your giant of fear. Then do it, boldly and courageously! Though your journey may lead you through cancer, divorce, addiction, or debt, God is with you everywhere you go!

Forgiveness. "You have a burr under your saddle," a trusted friend announced to my wife and me.

We had requested her input, but this came as a shock. We consider ourselves to be quite forgiving people! I had served as a minister and effectively been in the "grace business." Who was she to tell me about my need to forgive? As our conversations unfolded, we admitted that she was correct. We did have a burr under our saddle, and it was hindering us from a peaceful life.

Gary Chapman says it this way. "I am amazed at how many individuals mess up every new day with yesterday." [22] Thanks to a direct word from a friend, we decided to deal with that burr from yesterday.

As we processed what the source of our anger might be, we came to different conclusions. I needed to forgive myself for an excessive period of denial at the onset of my wife's illness. I had been a lousy caregiver. She, on the other hand, identified a particular person and a specific conversation. On her path of forgiveness, Kathy re-lived the intense emotions of the experience, began forgiving, and renewed communication with the individual.

A few weeks after that abrupt diagnosis, we had removed the burrs from under our saddles. Our long-held anger subsided, and newfound peace rushed in to fill that space as we continued to forgive.

In his book, *Forgive For Good,* Dr. Fred Luskin defines forgiveness as the feeling of peace that emerges as you take your hurt less personally, take responsibility for how you feel, and become a hero instead of a victim in the story you tell. [23]

To avoid facing this giant of forgiveness is to suffer unnecessarily. "Linger too long in the stench of your hurt, and you'll smell like the toxin you despise," says Max Lucado. [24] True. Grudges cause you to reek of a foul spirit.

To be sure, a key element in wrestling with forgiveness is re-writing your story. How will you continue to respond? Does this situation require a confrontation? Or is this a hurt that can be "let go?" One way or the other, you must refuse to be the victim, and instead take responsibility for re-writing your story.

Dr. Froma Walsh makes this important distinction. "Forgiveness is often confused with forgetting. Forgiving the *person* is confused with forgiving the *offense*." [25] Wrongdoing is not okay. The action itself will never be all right. But, as spiritual creatures we can learn to forgive the person and perhaps reconcile relationships.

As I have spoken with hundreds of caregivers through support groups and seminars, this sticking point of forgiveness always strikes a chord. Typically, caregivers struggle to forgive doctors for failed treatment plans, family members for insensitive remarks, and loved ones for failures in self-care. But most often, guilt-stricken caregivers grapple with the task of forgiving themselves; reluctant to afford themselves the grace they may easily afford others.

If you have been sick or addicted or drowning financially, you may be holding a grudge. If you have been losing a relationship or caring for a loved one or out of work, you may have a burr under your saddle. Your giant may be *forgiveness*.

To intentionally enter the upward spiral of forgiveness, these suggestions will lead you on a healthy path.

***

- Identify the grievance. Face it, and re-live it in great detail. Be very specific to recall names, times, actions and words that hurt.
- Determine any actions you need to take. Remember that you only have control over your own decisions; you cannot force the other party to do anything, nor do you need them to take any action for *you* to forgive them.
- Forgive the person. Deliberately and intentionally, release the person from your anger.

***

As Dr. Luskin explains, "Forgiveness is above all a choice." [26] My wife and I chose to face our giant of forgiveness. Since then, the ride has been much more enjoyable with no burrs under our saddles.

***

Maybe you share these giants of fear and forgiveness. Perhaps your giant is named doubt, discipline, laziness, selfishness, debt, or depression. Please take an important step in your journey to the resilient life by naming your giants, analyzing your past approach, and embarking on a future of facing your giants!

You can do it! God is with you. Your giant is no match for God!

Discovering Your Giants

1. What are the three giants you are facing (or are most likely to face)?

2. What have you done in the past?

3. What will you do this time?

Profile in Resilience: Rick Reed

April 6th, 2001, is a day that I will never forget. That day changed the course of my life for the better. It was on that day in Hitachi, Japan, that I found out that I had cancer. Stage 4 Non-Hodgkins lymphoma. That diagnosis would set me down the path to a newfound strength.

God has been so good to me even through the times that I felt like God wasn't there at all. Looking back I can see in so many ways that God was present. I have learned many lessons because of my cancer that have made me so much stronger than before. Going through all the chemo and eventually a stem cell transplant weakened other parts of my body, but my spirit has become much stronger.

True, there are days that I really want to go out and kick someone's butt in a game of basketball, but I just can't do that anymore. In fact, there was a time when I was so physically weak that when I fell I couldn't get back up. My legs were so weak that I had to depend on others to help me up. At one point, I weighed 135 pounds. I'm 6-4! Right now I'm still 6-4, but thankfully through many Sonic cherry vanilla Dr.Peppers, hamburgers, onion rings and many other delicious and fattening foods, I now weigh 170 pounds!

When battling cancer, you have two choices. You can enjoy the ride or complain. Believe me, there were times I did complain, but I also took time to enjoy the journey. These are the memories I look back and laugh at fondly.

For example, one fall I really wanted to go to a Halloween party. But, I didn't know what costume would possibly work. At the time, I was completely bald and I actually weighed 200 pounds. I had never weighed that much! So, I went as Uncle Fester from the Addams Family!

I remember fondly being able to play basketball when I had a month off before my stem cell transplant. I was bald and white as a ghost. But, I could still play! I thank God that I was able to have the time of being with my friends. I also enjoyed making my "Cancer Survivor" and "My Friend Is A Cancer Survivor" Japanese T-shirts. I got so bored during my treatments and with being unable to work that I came up with the T-shirt idea to have some type of income. I heard someone say once that God will use you because of you and He will use you in spite of you. I encourage you to live a resilient life and let God use you because of the circumstances in your life. No matter how difficult, God will use you anyway, and it might as well be because you want Him to!!!!

***

Rick Reed currently lives in Portland, Ore. If you would like to learn more about Rick or buy one of his T-shirts, go to www.shourishablogspot.com

Embracing Resilience

Never give up, for that is just the place and time that the tide will turn.

-Harriet Beecher Stowe

***

Lessons from a Cat

On the campus where I work, we have five buildings, about 100 employees...and a cat farm. Many, many cats, that finally resulted in many, many fleas. So, we decided it was time for the cats to go. Several tenderhearted employees took them home and then a cat-catching service came to get the rest. Except for one. One cat slipped by all of the traps, climbed up a tree and onto the outside second floor of one of our buildings to have a litter of kittens! We took pictures, sent them out on e-mail and generally admired this cat. The next morning, we discovered that after all the attention of the previous day, the cat and the kittens had somehow gotten back down the tree and taken up residence at an undisclosed location. A couple of days later, I happened to notice this momma cat and her kittens two blocks away at their new home (off of our cat-catching campus)!

This is a resilient cat! I think I agree with one employee's assessment of the situation, when she said that she wanted whatever DNA was in that cat! This one is a survivor. Resilient!

***

Your Birthright

After all of this talk about resilience, you may still not be convinced. "What if it's just not in my genes?" "What if I'm not made of that kind of stuff?" "Perhaps this is for other people, but not me." Stop it!

If these kinds of thoughts are pestering you, take a moment to rebuild. "Resilience can be defined as the capacity to rebound from adversity strengthened and more resourceful," according to Froma Walsh, who is perhaps the foremost researcher and scholar on the matter. [27]

Sure, by pursuing this path you may be bucking conventional wisdom's limiting line. And just because you are resilient, does not mean that you are not vulnerable to problems. Don't invite problems. But when they crop up, remember that you will be strong *in spite of* those problems and maybe even *because of* your difficulties.

If you have never yet experienced much resilience, you will be glad to know that several researchers have discovered that your early experiences in overcoming adversity do not determine your current experience and ability to bounce forward. You can develop resilience at any point in life, even if you have consistently failed in the past!

Resilience is your birthright!

***

The Resilient Family

As you personally embrace resilience, you must help your family onto this path as well. To this end, Nick Stinnett and John DeFrain have studied the strengths of more than 14,000 families in at least 27 countries. Their "Family

Strengths Model consists of six qualities which strong families across the world tend to share: commitment to the family; appreciation and affection for each other; positive communication patterns; enjoyable time together; a sense of spiritual well-being and connection; and the ability to successfully manage stress and crisis." [28]

Far and away, the most important of these is commitment. If you are living in a family system, your loved ones must know that your commitment to them is solid. As Joe Beam, author of *Fantastic Families*, states, "When each family member knows that the others are there and always will be there and that the family is above everything else — work, recreation, other people, crises, or whatever — that family has the ability to develop the other five characteristics that make them strong and happy. No one in a committed family lives in fear that he or she might be booted out or that some other family member will abandon them." [29]

None of us communicates perfectly or operates in a family system without some fault. But where there is commitment to each other and a gracious spirit, a family can learn to thrive.

In the face of trauma, misfortune, or transition, building a resilient family requires elasticity and buoyancy. [30] If you are currently in a difficult season as a family, your love will be tested. Yet, it is through this testing that you will discover your capacity for resilience.

***

God is with you

Now, some folks tend to experience life crashes and adopt that sad state of mind, commonly referred to as the "victim mentality." I remember one of the most important days in my wife's illness, when she resolutely informed me that she was not a "sick person." True, she has a disease that has not yet been cured or healed and that might even be with her for the rest of her life. But she was not about to be a "sick person," only ever feeling sorry for herself. She is choosing to be a resilient person, who also happens to deal with the inconveniences of a specific disease.

I have made poor choices in job transitions. But, those poor choices did not consign me to a life of failure. I have made poor financial choices in the past. Yet, I am not doomed to live my entire life as a financial failure. I have learned and changed. I was a lousy caregiver for awhile. But, I faced that reality, faced my giant, and become a much better caregiver for the good of my loved ones.

Whatever bad circumstances or even bad choices have produced less-than-ideal or perhaps catastrophic results in your life…these do not define you!

Joseph was a godly man and a godly leader…he just happened to take a unique career path. He was the same godly man as a hated brother, servant in Potiphar's house, and prisoner as he was as a national leader and gracious brother in the end. Joseph was resilient. And so are you!

***

Transcending Circumstance

Again, circumstances do not define you. Just because you have bombed out in your marriage, finances, or career, does not mean that you are finished. Likewise, the presence of disease, extended illness, or depression in your current experience cannot keep peace away from you forever.

Peace and hope are yours in abundance. Sure, we must deal with the facts of the situation and bear some consequences. But, God is not withholding peace or hope from you. In the midst of challenging circumstances, you can actually become more whole.

I meet these types of people all of the time. And I admire them deeply. People who care for loved ones who no longer remember their names. Individuals who have crashed at various times in life, and yet they speak of love, and faith, and hope. These unsung heroes encourage others with lesser plights. They freely and genuinely express gratitude. Along the way, these resilient people have released the notion of entitlement and receive every day as a gift. They are the people who transcend their circumstances!

The choices arrive daily. Sometimes the circumstances change, and sometimes they don't. As these words capture it, *sometimes God stills the storm to calm his frightened child. Sometimes he lets the storm rage, and calms his child instead.*

Every day that a person chooses to receive the abundant presence of God, something wonderful happens. Resilience takes place in and through and beyond circumstances.

***

So what?

If all of this is true, you will not only think of yourself as resilient, you will begin to act with resilience. Effectively, you will do what needs to be done.

As you do what needs to be done to face reality, face your giants, and enter the upward spiral of resilience, you will begin to accept your resilient identity. If you think of yourself as a resilient person, you will find more energy in the moment. One good thing feeds the other.

No matter how dire your current circumstances, you can begin to take small positive steps in the right direction to create new realities in your life! As it turns out, circumstances do not define you. Your response to those circumstances does. You are a resilient person! You have this capacity. Embrace it!

Discovering Your Own Resilience

1. How is your family or group of loved ones doing in each of these areas? What can you do to initiate good in a challenging area?

   Commitment:

   Expressing appreciation and affection:

   Sharing positive communication:

   Spending time together:

   Nurturing spiritual well-being:

   Coping with stress and crisis:

2. How would you rate yourself as a resilient person? (10=highest; 1=lowest)

3. Are you surprised to learn that resilient people are not exempt from problems? Who is one person that you consider to be resilient? What problems have they experienced? If you don't know, ask them. You may be surprised.

Helping Others

Greatness is not measured by how much you take, but by how much you give.

Anonymous

***

Surprised by "There"

AS YOU STEP INTO the groove of resilience, you may be shocked to find yourself serving again. You will not sit back, self-satisfied that you made it, hoping you never face another challenge. Rather, you will live the God-sized dream that puts you back in the God-sized battle. You will help other people once more!

The interesting thing about embracing resilience and helping others again is that after a crash, we identify so much better and so much more humbly with people. We move on from an "us serving them" mentality, to a higher, clearer vision of solidarity with all people. We have been to the bottom, so we're not so afraid to spend time with other people who have bottomed out.

I listened as a college student talked about being in a position of service, when she encountered a girl her own age whose life had taken a turn for more difficult circumstances and choices. I was so inspired by the mindset I heard, when this college student said, "You know, she's a girl just like me, with dreams just like me."

Resilient people don't look down on others for needing help, because resilient people are in touch with their own struggles. Therefore, they look people in the eyes and offer hope.

Other people aren't so scary. They're just like you, trying to find their way. You can help with that. You can provide pivotal help for someone else who is mired in adversity.

***

Maybe you're wondering what happened to Joseph — favorite son, fancy coat, beaten up, sold, accused of a crime, thrown in prison and forgotten. And yet, God was with Joseph all along, from interpreter of dreams and faithful servant to his becoming a national leader and gracious brother.

In the end, Joseph had as much reason and power as anyone who has ever lived to give up on God, to harbor resentment, and to get even. But Joseph was resilient. And this is what he says to the brothers who beat him and sold him, years later, when they were at his mercy and he had saved them from the famine years.

***

But Joseph told them, "Don't be afraid of me. Am I God, to judge and punish you? As far as I am concerned, God turned into good what you meant for evil. He brought me to the high position I have today so I could save the lives of many people. No, don't be afraid. Indeed, I myself will take care of you and your families." And he spoke very kindly to them, reassuring them.

-Genesis 50:19-21

***

Joseph completed the rhythm of God's reign. He embraced resilience and ultimately helped again by being a servant leader for a nation during seven years of famine. Then, he helped his brothers, by giving life to the very ones who wanted to take his.

***

Open My Eyes

You may find this hard to believe, but if you continue on the upward spiral of resilience, you will become a source of inspiration for someone who desperately needs your example. If this sounds a bit overwhelming, consider these words from Mother Teresa. "If I thought in terms of crowds, I would never begin my work. I believe in the personal touch of one to one." [31]

The power of one defies quantification. Your *one* story holds tremendous power to inspire people in similar situations, *one* at a time.

Kathy, my wife, carries the gift of encouragement. As college students, her notes of support endeared her to me. Come to find out, I wasn't the only one she encouraged. During our early years of marriage, I discovered that Kathy had the gift of hospitality as well. Listening, sharing hope, and believing in other people come easily to her.

About one year into her battle with Dermatomyositis, she informed me that perhaps her days of encouraging others were over. Her uneasy confession betrayed just how deeply she was hurting. For the next year, I occasionally affirmed that she had the gift of encouragement. Deep down, I knew what she could not yet see. She would help people struggling with long-term illnesses.

Two years later, she connected with a group of friends who had all experienced significant adversities. Building on their common pain, they formed a ministry of support for women living through similar life crashes. Through this ministry and countless individual conversations, *my wife is encouraging and helping people again!* She is credible because of her own struggles, and she shares hope with people who desperately need it.

***

Telling Your Story

On the journey to resilience, you will begin to tell *your* story of hope! *You* will become the person that other people look to and say, "If she has been through all of that and still shares hope, then so can I."

For many of you, *helping again* will go beyond simply telling your story. You will offer practical help to your neighbors and friends. You will listen. Some of you will form support groups and organizations. Others of you will raise awareness and funding. A few may even influence key legislation, and kick-start positive change that affects many lives. In whatever useful ways you begin to help people, your ability to do so will start with telling your story!

But in order to do so effectively, you need to learn to tell your story well. Please, don't tell your story of "no hope." Though well-intentioned, people who share a whiny, victim-based account of their adversity do not inspire us. They depress us.

At some point, most of us have done this. When we are in the brutal throes of a life crash, it is difficult not to tell a depressing story. If this is where you currently reside, only tell your story to those who can handle it. But as you progress on your journey to resilience, you will learn a new language and a new perspective on what has happened.

You will know that you are ready to share your story when you can end by imparting hope to the listener. True, your story will likely involve tragic events and may be heart-wrenching. You may cry. That's fine. This is reality. But if your purpose is to help another person, don't leave them depressed and feeling sorry for you. Tell the truth, and leave them with hope! We need to hear that story!

Learning to tell your story

1. What are the 5-10 most significant moments in your life crash (good and bad)?

2. Where is the hope? What good can you find?

3. How have faith, love, peace, joy, and patience played a role thus far?

4. What is the point of your story? If you could only speak one sentence to another person to help them, what would you say?

5. Now, practice telling your story in 10 minutes or less. Seriously. You may have opportunity for more, but economize. Most people can't stand to listen for much longer than this. Write out the most important sentences, and practice your 10 minutes that will probably be the hope someone needs!

Entering the Upward Spiral of Resilience

What we play is life.

-Louis Armstrong

***

BECOMING A RESILIENT PERSON does not exempt you from problems. Neither does it mean that you must be perfect. As Anna Quindlen says, "What is really hard, and really amazing, is giving up on being perfect and beginning the work of becoming yourself." [32] Your best self will be resilient, not perfect. Your best self is emerging *because of* problems, not because of the *absence of* problems.

In my home, Oklahoma City, stands a tree that inspires hundreds of people every day. This resilient American Elm has been identified in pictures from about 100 years ago. The tree has seen it all. Wide open space, the emergence of a city, good and evil.

On a spring day in 1995, I was working for a publishing company in downtown Oklahoma City. While on the phone with a professor from a university in California, I heard a loud boom. Our building shook, windows blew out, and I immediately explained that something terrible had just happened. As you have probably guessed, the date was April 19th. The event was the Oklahoma City bombing, which took 168 lives.

Eleven years later, we moved back to Oklahoma City. I finally mustered up the courage to visit the Memorial site. And there, standing grandly on the northern bank of the reflective pool, was that old American Elm.

The Survivor Tree.

This famed tree was initially filled with debris from the blast and almost cut down, until a group of people decided to help nurture it back to health. Today, the Survivor Tree thrives and inspires many people to embrace resilience.

Sometimes I visit the tree, just to ponder the inherent capacity for resilience that resides in all of creation. I have witnessed resilience in the people of Oklahoma City. I have discovered this gift in my own family tree. And I have increasingly embraced resilience in my own life.

You hold this same capacity! Not because you are invincible or immune to problems. Rather, you are resilient because you were created that way. Mahatma Gandhi puts it this way. "We may not be God, but we are of God."[33] This coincides with the "doctrine of Immanence that grace emanates out from the God within the center of man's being."[34] Or, you might say, "God in us and us in God."

With this view of ourselves and with a little help from our friends, we can survive any crisis of adversity and even live to help others!

The journey to resilience begins with facing reality. You must tell the brutal truth about your situation. Then, seek to understand your system. What can you learn about yourself, your family, your conflict style? Again, what is the truth about your circumstances?

With a firm grounding in reality, you are set to dream. But remember, don't just dream me-sized dreams, ask to receive God-sized dreams! As God is faithful in granting dreams, so will God be with you as you plan again.

Of course, just about the time you get your dreams and plans together, some giant will raise its ugly head. You must face your giant! From God's perspective, the giant really is no match.

If you can travel this far in the journey, you are ready to embrace resilience. Sure, you will encounter more adversity and need to face new and difficult realities in the future. But having experienced your own capacity for resilience, you will remember the deep joy of doing the right thing!

As a resilient person, bouncing forward from a life crash, you are equipped to live the greatest dream: helping others. Many people need to hear your story of hope, and receive your help to enjoy the gift of resilience in their own lives!

You can do it! Today is your day! You can begin living in the upward spiral of the resilient life! The gift is yours. Receive it and live it. As I write these final words, I pray that you will move with determination from bitter reality to resilient living!

Entering the Upward Spiral of Resilience

1. Drawing from your answers in previous chapters, complete your intentional plan for resilient living.
   - My reality, right now:
   - My newest understanding about my system or family:
   - My God-sized dream:
   - My God-sized plan:
   - My giant:

- My biggest sign of embracing resilience:

- My way to help others:

- Sure signs that I am entering the upward spiral of resilience:

2. Someone you know is experiencing a life crash. If this resource has been helpful to you, please share it with them. Write the name of the person below and pray for an opportunity to help them live the resilient life!

Resources

Coaching

For personal, couple or family coaching on any of the following topics, go to www.myresilientlife.com to learn more or to request an initial evaluation.

Diagnostic Tools

Conflict

Discover Your Conflict Management Style (Book), Speed B. Leas, 1997.

http://peace.mennolink.org/resources/conflictstyle/styles.html

Family

www.thebowencenter.org

www.prepare-enrich.com

www.familydynamics.org

Personality

www.authentichappiness.sas.upenn.edu

www.humanmetrics.com

www.myersbriggs.org

www.smalleyonline.com

Stress

www.caregiverstress.com

www.drrahe.com

http://health.discovery.com/centers/stress/assessments/stress_assessment.html

Disease Specific Information Sources

www.alz.org	Alzheimer's Disease
www.parkinson.org	Parkinson's Disease
www.nami.org	Mental Illness
www.americanheart.org	Heart/Stroke
www.cancer.org	Cancer
www.mayoclinic.org	For reliable information on almost all other diseases

Family Caregivers

www.caregiver.com	*Today's Caregiver* Magazine
www.caringtoday.com	*Caring Today* Magazine
www.caregiver.org	Family Caregiver Alliance
www.nfcacares.org	National Family Caregivers Association
www.wellspouse.org	Well Spouse Association

Financial Resources

www.daveramsey.com Dave Ramsey's resources to get out of debt

Other Tools

http://psychologytoday.com/topics/addiction.html Addiction
www.48days.com Dan Miller's Career Overhaul resource

For more information about *Resilient Life* resources, go to: www.MyResilientLife.com

To schedule Bruce McIntyre for a seminar or keynote address, please make your initial request by e-mail to: info@MyResilientLife.com

For book orders:

Online:

www.MyResilientLife.com

By e-mail:

info@MyResilientLife.com

NOTES

Chapter 1: Facing Reality

[1] Froma Walsh, *Strengthening Family Resilience* (New York: The Guilford Press, 2006), ix.
[2] John 8:32.
[3] Walsh, *Strengthening Family Resilience*, 16.
[4] Beth Witrogen McLeod, *Caregiving: The Spiritual Journey of Love, Loss, and Renewal* (New York: John Wiley and Sons, Inc., 1999), 1.
[5] M. Scott Peck, *The Road Less Traveled* (New York: Simon and Schuster, 1978), 30.
[6] Peck, *The Road Less Traveled*, 16.
[7] Dr. Charles Siburt, *Managing Conflict in Churches Class Notebook*, (2001), 355.
[8] Peck, *Road Less Traveled*, p. 64.

Chapter 2: Understanding Your System

[9] Taken from the work of Dr. Gary Smalley and Dr. John Trent. This information is taken from a handout provided by Dr. Gary Smalley in a seminar in Searcy, Ark., in 1997. Please check their resources at www.smalleyonline.com or www.strongfamilies.com for more help and ideas.
[10] Taken from a talk by Dr. Gary Smalley. Please check www.smalleyonline.com for more great resources.
[11] William Bridges, *Transitions* (Reading, Mass.: Addison-Wesley Publishing Company, 1980), 9.
[12] Granger E. Westberg, *Good Grief* (Philadelphia: Fortress Press, 1971).

Chapter 3: Dreaming Again

[13] Walsh, *Strengthening Family Resilience,* 55.
[14] www.Rubelshelley.com/content.
[15] I have a forthcoming book on this very topic, *The Best News I Never Heard*. If you would like to receive coaching to help you through this spiritual stumbling block, check www.myresilientlife.com for information on my coaching services.
[16] Thomas Merton, *The Seven Storey Mountain* (San Diego: Harcourt Brace and Company, 1998), 187.

[17] Bruce Wilkinson, *The Dream Giver* (Sisters, Ore.: Multnomah, 2003), 73-75.

Chapter 4: Planning Again

[18] Lewis Carroll, *Alice in Wonderland,* adapted by Susan Linney (New York: Modern Publishing, 2005), 89-91.
[19] Taken from a book title by Brian McLaren and Tony Campolo, *Adventures in Missing the Point.*
[20] Eugene Peterson, *A Long Obedience in the Same Direction: Discipleship in an Instant Society,* (Intervarsity Press, 2000).

Chapter 5: Facing Your Giants

[21] Walsh, *Strengthening Family Resilience,* 14-15.
[22] Gary Chapman, *The Five Love Languages* (Chicago: Northfield Publishing, 2004), 47.
[23] Fred Luskin, *Forgive for Good* (New York: HarperCollins Publishers, Inc., 2002), vii.
[24] Max Lucado, *Facing Your Giants* (Nashville: W Publishing Group, 2006), 25.
[25] Walsh, *Strengthening Family Resilience,* 350.
[26] Luskin, *Forgive for Good,* 217.

Chapter 6: Embracing Resilience

[27] Walsh, *Strengthening Family Resilience,* 4.
[28] Simone Silberberg, "Searching for Family Resilience," *Family Matters* 58 (Autumn 2001), 52.
[29] Joe Beam, *Fantastic Families* (West Monroe, La.: Howard Publishing, 1999), 17.
[30] www.cyfernet.org/research/resilient.html.

Chapter 7: Helping Others

[31] Mother Teresa, *In My Own Words* (Liguori, Mo.: Liguori Publications, 1996), 99.

Chapter 8: Entering the Upward Spiral of Resilience

[32] Anna Quindlen, *Being Perfect*, (New York: Random House, 2005), 15.
[33] M.K. Ghandi, *The Way to God* (Berkeley, Calif.: Berkeley Hills Books, 1999), 40.
[34] Peck, *The Road Less Traveled,* 261.

You have the capacity for resilience!